www.finishinglinepress.com

kyrie eleison or
all robins taken out of context

poems by

Debasis Mukhopadhyay

Finishing Line Press
Georgetown, Kentucky

kyrie eleison or
all robins taken out of context

poems by

Debasis Mukhopadhyay

Finishing Line Press
Georgetown, Kentucky

kyrie eleison or
all robins taken out of context

to Rustam, my jigar tala

ACKNOWLEDGMENTS

I would like to thank the editors of the following journals & anthologies, in which
many of these poems, often in different versions, first appeared : *Algebra of Owls,
Erbacce, I Am Not a Silent Poet, Mannequin.Haüs, Scarlet Leaf Review, The Curly
Mind, The New Verse News, Thirteen Myna Birds, With Painted Words, Words
Dance, Writers Against Prejudice.*

Publisher: Leah Maines

Editor: Christen Kincaid

Cover Art: Carol Radsprecher, www.carolradsprecher.com

Author Photo: Vivek Swarup

Cover Design: Elizabeth Maines McCleavy

Printed in the USA on acid-free paper.
Order online: www.finishinglinepress.com
          also available on amazon.com

Author inquiries and mail orders:
Finishing Line Press
P. O. Box 1626
Georgetown, Kentucky 40324
U. S. A.

Table of Contents

What man could travel this long road & not fill up his soul with crazy arabesques? Who would dare say "I walked along a path in my head, & it wasn't a path for birds or for fish or for men, but a path for our ears"?

— Lorca

What man could travel this long road & not fill up his soul with crazy arabesques? Who would dare say "I walked along a path in my head, & it wasn't a path for birds or for fish or for men, but a path for our ears"?

— Lorca

kyrie eleison, or a surplus of fallen robins

yes i am that old trombonist who sees death / dangling in every bird

every day a surplus of fallen robins dart around under the rubble of my daydreaming

the more i hear the clunk of their lost wings the more my notes become / glowworms illuminating the intact ribs of children in whispering tremolo

many a times i try to play serenely half-notes with dotted rests revealing / their immortal bones under the rubble / perhaps /

the wavering melody gives the impression of an ivory creek of misplaced optimism / or just of some theoretical tulips blubbing inside a cylindrical museum of war

& i play euphonium thinking the bromide nuance of my embouchure might help you with the surmise that the sinew of those fallen birds is a bright mercurial descent of a starry night traveling past a mortuary

you are my half-brother half-fruitcake half-misdeal half-nirvana / tell me where have you hidden those deaf-aid reverse tracks of death / between redness & cinders between the mortuary of Monte Carlo & the museum of war of Luxembourg ain't no frank blood

neither in Syria where with a puckered smile i play highlife in tuba

the more i play the more a sheen on that rubble of my daydreaming turns kidney color or if you like sun-bleached lilac / o overwintering flowers go fuck yourselves in your fast-draining soil

an elegy for the flayed ox

bones splinter down the roads

like they do
       here
              here
&
       where
              your breath
       cuts
thoughts
to
tendril out
from congealed blood

&
       dragonflies
       come out
of the river of lullabies
like drones
         at
sundown

bobbing upon
peeled bodies

watching
an embalmed sky
       its
arcane capillaries
toward a vanishing blue

where
chalk breaks
into pieces
&
melts
in our fingers
& waits
to circle the world

the narrow skull of Aylan Kurdi

hand me
those marbles
rolling down
          the map
        heavy
under my skin
            marbles
marbles
all mistaken for stars
bucking the seas
mistaken for skies
blue seven-knot skies
that my narrow skull
keeps swallowing
          they egress
& fall through
the skin   home
wrinkling

back home
i was a doll
who would sleep like a doll
nothing more
          nothing more
in the nights of
barrel bombs

if you are here papa
haul down those stars
or throw them back

penny for your thoughts

i am not a bird that flies
          just
an un-alone head
that lies low & heavy

to dispute its trading

still buried in the foxholes

it's about a namesake / navel or nasturtium / needle or necessity / narcissus or napalm / just trying to slash up the words like thistle heads / a bloody poem / such jubilance of your mirth bursting out of the masquerade / a flunkey like me needs to withhold the eyes of a songbird / will i lose you to the biological worms if i ever sing you / your hairline / the mended hem around your *tabula rasa* curling up in the final bluing / over five hundred miles i can think along the same lines as Beckett / Godot / no / Godot maybe next / in the glass it's just strewn dust of flesh languishing in a landscape that smells of a roasted map of Syria / o flowering or must i say narrowing now / the bee will hum around your skull as long as i try to obliterate the ghosts the candid oblivion laid down in my youth / today all their groans are still buried in the foxholes here & there inside me / you have to squeeze them hard to hear *never again pogrom never again* a bowing skeleton without a country / is a line of rosettes shining across a crystalline barbed wire mere disgrace as a poem / a poem never asks you for rosy eyes when it hatches out like a precocial chick / not a single word / just lay down your eye sockets discrowned / there will be beetroots & hummingbirds making just another poem of half-moon eyes

the sum of empty holes

this bullet so smashed up against the anterior margin of my eye socket
time & time again i heard bullets blaring abruptly inside bony walls
leaving silence slick muffled by water
i thought this one would be shuffling out of the ocular globe without a
hitch
at least it would fear to lose itself to darkness like a baby girl
& try its luck outside the hollow
it stayed right there rooted to the loading dock bleeding
like the shadow of a gull beating
down upon the stillness of earth
this bullet brought raspberry color rills but no scent
yes i have a right to be optimistic about the world even though
i harbored false hope about the upside-down bullet
this one won't ever know the expanding circles of dazzle
underneath my icicled skin
this one will just remain as a smashed up daisy easy to remember
in the days we play chess in black & white

telescope & night ornaments

through the trap door of the night sky the telescope
brings you the debris of a million suns
shimmering on a canvas you liked all along
the bright night of Van Gogh crawls into your eyes
& makes you forget that bone color priming can also be
grown into a moonlit canvas (like History)
everything in the underpainting is meant to be painted over
the manna of bombs that astound the bodies with brightness
& the bodies that gather in the pit
waiting to grow wings of no consequence
yes but everything in the dead coloring is intended
to be painted over
to swallow such brightness in your canvas
you can paint the clouds that ring my brother's skull
into an hourglass that swells lolling on my mother's chest
there is no blood between her breasts
doves just coo & sugar ants lick all witness
she pauses to dream
the dreams that look into the muddy darkness beneath your feet
for night ornaments built for tomorrows or yesterdays

menos tu vientre
after Miguel Hernandez

she knows
Hope
just said
footfalls & wings
the broken kind
always undoing the hasp
tugging endless
tongues
that'd played & honeyed
lofty sorrows
of silk
laid over blue nails

absence
absence
absence
borne away
in a scant light

rosewood beads
around the neck
around nothing
molting
the tang of longing
your belly
your belly
your belly

she knows
the nest hollowed out
& nails hammered into
the hatchlings
always blind & naked
such moist evenings
huddle closer in the weight of bones
brightened by bombs

spindrifts
awaiting in the beauty
of the broken field of cries
always bending upon
the bayonets
tossing lopsided roads
to her incised map
to terraform
memories
clogged
between
translucent rubble & roadkill

& her starry nights
would narrate *Amel* in life
over the crust of the bleeding
marauder in her womb
stars' egress
sultry blubber
& biography
cracking up
billowing

Amel
Amel
Amel

she knows
shrapnel that hides her eyes
hides the sea in a fold
such an old word
Hope
never said before
ruthless blood shifting
borders
& infinity

she has got spine
swimming across the serrated
fence to make appear
a skein of birds
to be a hem of calligraphy
alighting in her gunshot belly
what has yet to come
grazed
by her blue fingers
every time a ticker
seems at work
in a bare paradise
stippling the nights
a strobe of
baby skulls
cry
tu vientre
tu vientre
menos tu vientre
your belly   your belly
except for your belly

everything else is dark

———————

"[L]ast week, in Aleppo [,] a newborn named Amel, or 'Hope,'
came into the world bearing a piece of shrapnel in her forehead."
[CNN] September 24, 2015.

a zebra i want to write a zebra

an array of upturned coffins keeling over an indigo road
leads me to the border
maybe i should try to write a spine
the sunrays in the spine quieted like melancholia yet still
glinting through cobwebs over the kingdoms of the killings
sunshine yes but i would probably keep the sunshine aside
& thousands of its likelihoods
thinking of the ripples of weapons murmuring
like a saline breeze around our best immediate interest
fingers perhaps growing sunflowers
fingers not bloodied smudging the pastel until a hallow appears
lodged in the hollow songs
freshly hatched out of the muskets
fingers wrap us in a musical of red poppies
glimmering in the sun beneath the water
are myriad skulls weighing down the long drowned boats
the sea is known to be turbulent at times
think of the firmament
under those naked skins the firmament
keeps gazing on the slalom of lives awaiting a starry Lych gate
& with all the starlets dripping fireballs in the mind
i open a lifespan of lullabies for the children of war
dreams only root from dreams & their shambles roll
across the rubbed pastel debris to shatter against
your silhouette of folly
oh muse mine what is there to write?
sail on doll head sail on
the night is your wool of time your doom your lilac womb
go go fetch a zebra

between ink & inkblot

through the branches i ease the sky
leaves
birds
songs
nada nada
beneath the hollow
Chinese ink
spackles over
a daub of spring & a cherry tree
clasped in each other

this was all i hoped for

now about ink & inkblot
the excavations from boneyards dated back to 256 BC
suggest
kneading was used
to invent ink
& to evolve back to tomorrow

i draw a last warm breath
that sips
a gleam of
blood waiting
to belong
in the cracks
that crowd to my eyes

i think
before
i soot those hide glued eyes

"Ink, whose semantic component is 'earth', is black." wrote Xu Schen
(58 CE – ca. 147 CE)

Birobidzhan, or one day in the life of Jose Maria

rain falls on the fecund smell of the bay
on the salty pebbles of Santa Barbara
& devours the lullabies
which could perhaps still kindle your bones
it's never enough Jose Maria
to confess dreams
a reindeer skull held in thrall
emptied of its sad blood for evermore
what's left these days is the shadow
of footfalls seeping down
the loose spine
playing a hymn you heard for the first time
in Birobidzhan
where the Trans-Siberian railroad
wavered & died away
in the ripples of Bira
swallowing the patina of sky
where the engine smoke
lay forever in the tangle of slated roofs
& bell towers
lofty walls & crossroads
your longing inscribed in a sepia postcard
tresses falling over
the gypsy girl's shoulders
who laughed while making love
to you
who thought the best thing
to do before the pogroms
loomed closer
was to exorcise the stars
above our graves
Ivanushka was never her real name

today in the sunroom
Jose Maria

a train of shadows passes you hull down
in a flightless air
wrapping & unwrapping
time & clime congealed in your lungs
like a lump of light or a flower-lit stream
aiming to unleash the soul
to resound blindly
one day
such long waiting in hope
like watching the jiggers
burrow blindly head-first into your skin
breathing defecating
& expelling eggs
time is nothing flecked with eyes
all around your suspended skull
a noble skull for how-to-draw-a-cubist-still life
i always thought
cut flowers wane under your eyes
still helmed in
a mud-moon
spurting above forlorn Birobidzhan
yet to surmise its own doom
the leg of lamb crumples tenderly
to the flame in the oven
the first & last time you prayed
you said i am lost
perhaps another cup of cocoa
perhaps another smuggled cigar
& no funneling back
to the nights of broken glass
perhaps it's never enough
to go on asking
time is nothing a streak of light
over a slashed pomegranate
a cubist still life i always thought
a ravenous skull

the dreams pounding on your bald pate
Jose Maria
wherever you touch earth
your meaty lovers will come
from the hollow of the map of the world
& kiss you on your eyes
glimpsed scene by scene
the memories vomited from their stomachs
wherever you touch earth
the carnival queen will come
out of the hollow
of your flesh to exhume then forsake her love
leaving you a voice that appears as if
"air has been trapped in the stomach & forced through the mouth
after being out of water"
something that a lobster does in the boil
something that those who flooded the camps
didn't do
clamouring like burning tulips

you wish you had known
a home
a woman
a riverbed of incandescent sky
instead of a memorial train
taking you again & again
inside a diagram
of transitive earth where the stations float up
backward & rains
keep on oiling the metal wheels
of your train loaded with the then Jews
(something we all can relate
to our best childhood movies)
their heads rolled off
to sleep in a webbing of dried blood

for years to come
crashing onto the shingle of their longings
time is nothing
the train keeps coming back
crawling through your eye sockets
like dreams you wish
scooped out of your skull
for a day or two

time is nothing
a Jew is a Jew is a Jew
singing singing
the map of the world flies open
wherever you touch earth
all the places are warped trying to curl
you wish you could have found
their bones falling
by the cattle cars
still warbling unperturbed

rain falls on the salty grapes
Jose Maria
mounted on your Picasso's hat
the women you met in Vienna
dangled in a party shop
like pendula
not suspecting the coming years
ticktock ticktock
women reflected in the polished parquetry
in Paris
like lighted candles foretelling
the coming years
ticktock ticktock
time is never the depths
between the soft mounds
of those creatures

the everlasting is the curved staircase
God betroths you
in a vermilion twilight of clouds
if you pay the price
to collapse in the arms of a china doll
knowing in your heart
you will die like a Jew someday
in a mute canvas
like a mistake resounding beneath
the rabbit skin glue
clenching death with both hands

the words you would have trafficked
all through your life
like a poet
under your breath
living & dreaming of the passage
of days in Birobidzhan
with the wounded conscience
of a smuggler of burned potatoes
awaiting a reckless wind
breaking into a cold sweat inside his sonnets
awaiting a slanting rain
to press on his burning stones

you are that poet
walking backward from Birobidzhan
to a dream-squandered sky
you are that souvenir
bending over an open grave
to bid rejoice
ha   blessed the skull
folly to this still life
still-untitled
or
a bleached deer skull
antlers awakened out of dreams

watching is harder than asphyxiation
in memory of Quandeel Baloch (Fauzia Azeem)

blue poppies all around my music box
no blood no puddle no songs
just my tight skin
that you thought i owed you
with my mouth & nose pinned shut
i let you watch
my ocean blue cotton shirt circling into the dark tipped nipples
of my two worlds of flesh

yes my mouth still feels parched now
as if i'm in between loves
how long has it been
aimlessly transporting my head filled with
young coconut water
it's an odd time when you can get out of your mind
to say something like this
you didn't have a chance to stop the blue silhouette
of your hands weaving
thousand bracts & clusters of bougainvilleas
that you didn't know would scramble
over my bare shoulders with their spiky black tipped thorns
later they would tell you
we all know watching is harder than asphyxiation

i was asleep & dreaming under my skin
just like a *gul-e-nargis*
lashing the sky
no gravity no teetering yet no wings
just your big paws brother mine
& your dwarf cock risen puffing out
the family pride
you ain't no peacock
yet were you not a proud one then adorned with ugly claws
or did i just hear a peacock's harsh cry
filling the empty bones of life

& i ain't no oyster
just a gauzy slut
yet was i not an oyster then
squirming & wriggling under the lemon
come on brother
smothering an oyster misses the point
i let you peek in to
the deep of my hull where periods & honors
were unwritten

Quandeel Baloch (Fauzia Azeem), the 26 years old Pakistani model, actress, feminist activist & social media star, was asphyxiated on July 15, 2016 by her own brother in Pakistan for "bringing disrepute to the family's honour." Every year, nearly 1000 women are killed by their close relatives in "honor" cases in Pakistan.

death and other litanies

i want to go home / she said again / home ... home ... home / echoes brought paper cuts spinning in monochrome / the mist of Lima breaking open the ruby skin of crushed flowers lying on morning roads & i picked up those scattered clumps thinking i would keep a log of your death / then came pigeons rolling with silent waves of soiled sea looking for my stray words / the shiny bits & chunks of school girls' laughter made me think that childhood was a glass jar breaking into pieces of light / walking past the park i heard one i saying to another i / *you... you.... you .../* so many *you(s)* / & i could not have the chance to call her *you*

the windswept pictures looked under the darkroom safelight as amber as your father's submerged hope / there was light still clinging to those pictures of our fingers immersed in the stop bath of how-do-you-cope with it / night in the alleys of Cusco does not spoil you with any more sky than the narrowed eyes of your life / did you know when they handed you over to good hands of hospice care / one afternoon / i can still see the sun smile over the pool of spilled cranberry flow / the blushing catheter bag hanging under your electric bed / i travelled with you as if just to keep a log of withering heights / damn / the more you laughed the more your eyes were where sky seeks the swan of mind / when i walked up to Machu Picchu / green was a better word for a desert of ruins / it had never meant hope

what is will / you asked & the faces awaiting your will to will made a face / so you did ask again peering into their stare / *what is will without me* / & the hovering faces could not see the fluttering wings of butterflies you still could over the ruins / *but you...you are going to die ... realize it now / will you Miss* / the white doctor draped in ocean blue came worried thrice a week to wake you from your will to live / *i can't... & how can i doctor / the i is another / but remains still the i / & so where is that you to whom i can say / the way you tell me / you're going to die of your own death / oh Miss / travel / may be you can catch up with that missing you* / the echo filled the afternoon before fading into my log / *you... you.... you...* again many *you(s)* were casting their skin / i wondered whether i could call her in my missing you / *tell me / is the mountain of seven colors really a seven-color mountain* / you asked turning your head at me / & i could hear the geysers of red Altiplano rolling on the haze of when it becomes a desert / *there ain't no seven colors / no... no* / & we all came out of the home of hospice care shaking our rumbling heads as though we were just upset with her quest for colors & not with her lust for life

but for the ocean of shadows of Lake Titicaca where's blue in this landlocked country / i said showing you my pictures of the spinning clouds of silver over Copacabana / *true / no blue elsewhere in your ruby planet* / you said reeling with morphine & decadron / *but shadows keep wandering under those burning clouds / yes / i can imagine many of them chasing a fugue* / your smile unwound before me / the falling shadows of the bowler hats of Aymara & Quechua women & their ballads of russet dirt roads / *mi cholita* / said your Balkan friend locking you in her arms / *i can't write your diary anymore / it aches to be tangled with all the 'i's of yours i transcribe in there / i become lonelier being with those 'i's of yours than i would be tomorrow without you / the more i perpetuate with my pen the words of your 'i's / the more i become like a blue shadow what the evening will recede into*

shadow / what shadow when hope is so soiled in the body / i thought weaving the last words in the gloom of my log / sun was filling the room / in fact / sun was making room for the shadow of hospice care / there was no blue in there either / cinerarias alone were blooming as a prelude to the tolling bells of Poe in the scorching sun / sweetie / you said to her in allegro agitato / *hold me / & hold me please close to the sun*

how far are we really from Havana?

tell me how far are we really from Havana

i hate poisoning but i always forget / when you invited me thinking we ought to drink to my obliging cross / i looked through the window / the damp birds looked brighter along Malecon / you said forget simply forget / & the far off tomorrows seemed suddenly washed away / the album *America's National Parks* that lay unopened on the table of Floridita was turning into tender smoke one could see across the frenzied flesh of all those cats sitting on the extreme edge of the cornice with their belief in the sweet lethargy of gravity / the *guyabita del pinar* came in an oval jar as if bringing my death of my own accord & i asked again tell me are we really a long way from Havana forgetting i hate poisoning / you sighed over the bay of porkbelly juice & whispered / forget forget the hollow / & the lips streaming with bloodied saliva across the spiderweb of the CIA

i opened the vault & glanced back at the prerevolutionary maps of this island gleaming ninety miles away from the aurora americana / in each alley the everlasting dome of taciturn biographies was muttering bloody Providence or maybe Hosannah Hosannah / i peered helplessly into a dark cavern where the lonely crabs were crawling along the bare elbows of Che in search of a lyre / & like a criminal i was drawn to a miniscule Castro caught in a fishing net gloriously discarded by all lesson books studied in Jose Marti primary schools / i tried to gaze with the help of a sunburnt lantern flaring more & more brightly only to discover the amputated hands of Che amassing folk songs for tourist ladies like you senorita / don't just reiterate *hasta la victoria siempre siempre* / tell me why are you so quiet to your bird of prey?

the blue ham of the *bocadito* resembled the motionless thick smiles you granted me on my birthdays / forgive me i said out of trepidation / i don't want to go home / my fluffy verse can linger / & darling just forget there is no such window through which you can hear the Malecon / just try to look at the bottom where i have kept the oblivion still rosy / i told you what could be also your own words / i hate poisoning / sorry i am so insolent what can i do / i followed the path of dragonflies lifeless or just bitter if you like / & your lips moist with *canchanchara* muttered forget / forget dreaming / see your shoes are chirping away / & i howled / hail thee Cinderella / i swear i remember for the hundredth time i was limping alone up the Calle Muralla to the Plaza Vieja where the guns were leveled at my head / behind the wall of cries of hate of the spectators you can still hear me now knocking / La Habana La Habana

Lorca's body will never be found

clouds / clouds only flash past the waters at Kennebunkport / i'm learning to listen to the clank of the wild roses which are not my business / i can't write enough though my memories bark at my heels ever since i woke up in a cabin not far from the Dock square / where last night a kind of green of something gossamery near the windowsill was hankering for the warm breath of the stars through the rips of a sultry sky

& yes with a new name / not forgetting my old bitter name / i was thinking of the merriment promised behind the yellow door left ajar / the lamps & my memories gleaming enough to untangle my heart sleeping through the *duende* / so doomed yet trim & jaunty / my heart finally floated / last night at every bend of the Kennebunk River the drunken boat of Lorca wandered my way

thinking of Lorca i asked myself / should not i bequeath everything to emptiness of the rental cabin including the blue hyacinth grapes stirring from the numb depths of my white Christian bondage / before i pay for the boat? / the ceiling was descending / ecstasy dipped into emptiness / into salt / into half of an eye throbbing / i had known the yoke / fog's tenor slinking through the potion of hope / everything which sounds & resounds the gulp-choke melancholy of high tide in Ginsberg's America / & now it was the boat knocking knocking on that yellow door beckoning me

what was i thinking then / does America beget more than America? / my face must have looked marred by an inscrutable masquerade / no? / no / not my face / it was Lorca's wax soft forehead shimmering in the *duende* i have been carrying all through my life / *welcome to the stage* / i heard his insistent verse ringing out / without drawing a breath i knew the oleanders were asking forgiveness for their old bitterness potted in blood / tonight i will walk the path with them until i get to the boat / *trade me if you like for your laments* / Lorca said inside my skull /

Lorca's body will never be found

clouds / clouds only flash past the waters at Kennebunkport / i'm learning to listen to the clank of the wild roses which are not my business / i can't write enough though my memories bark at my heels ever since i woke up in a cabin not far from the Dock square / where last night a kind of green of something gossamery near the windowsill was hankering for the warm breath of the stars through the rips of a sultry sky

& yes with a new name / not forgetting my old bitter name / i was thinking of the merriment promised behind the yellow door left ajar / the lamps & my memories gleaming enough to untangle my heart sleeping through the *duende* / so doomed yet trim & jaunty / my heart finally floated / last night at every bend of the Kennebunk River the drunken boat of Lorca wandered my way

thinking of Lorca i asked myself / should not i bequeath everything to emptiness of the rental cabin including the blue hyacinth grapes stirring from the numb depths of my white Christian bondage / before i pay for the boat? / the ceiling was descending / ecstasy dipped into emptiness / into salt / into half of an eye throbbing / i had known the yoke / fog's tenor slinking through the potion of hope / everything which sounds & resounds the gulp-choke melancholy of high tide in Ginsberg's America / & now it was the boat knocking knocking on that yellow door beckoning me

what was i thinking then / does America beget more than America? / my face must have looked marred by an inscrutable masquerade / no? / no / not my face / it was Lorca's wax soft forehead shimmering in the *duende* i have been carrying all through my life / *welcome to the stage* / i heard his insistent verse ringing out / without drawing a breath i knew the oleanders were asking forgiveness for their old bitterness potted in blood / tonight i will walk the path with them until i get to the boat / *trade me if you like for your laments* / Lorca said inside my skull /

the blue ham of the *bocadito* resembled the motionless thick smiles you granted me on my birthdays / forgive me i said out of trepidation / i don't want to go home / my fluffy verse can linger / & darling just forget there is no such window through which you can hear the Malecon / just try to look at the bottom where i have kept the oblivion still rosy / i told you what could be also your own words / i hate poisoning / sorry i am so insolent what can i do / i followed the path of dragonflies lifeless or just bitter if you like / & your lips moist with *canchanchara* muttered forget / forget dreaming / see your shoes are chirping away / & i howled / hail thee Cinderella / i swear i remember for the hundredth time i was limping alone up the Calle Muralla to the Plaza Vieja where the guns were leveled at my head / behind the wall of cries of hate of the spectators you can still hear me now knocking / La Habana La Habana

the mouth of the Kennebunk River was full of darkness churning
/ where did go the eroded sky-borne moon / my bones sealing
moon on a fresco in another life

the midnight's sirens prayed harder for America's hope dressed as
a striped woman with kohled eyelashes & a body of clay swollen
up on the bridge painted superfluous blue &/or red / which always
leap sweetly upon themselves in the presidential hullabaloo / i was
left face to face with a gaudy rhetoric of power asking me / *are you
ready? are you ready?* / as if i was just entitled to an interlude

& it was about time in Sodom / i didn't know if i had time to
remember the nymph i had left behind in an essentialist boat shop
gone down the drain / or the feigned shock in her waxy eyes /
when i anointed my hand in the cold sweat cauterizing her muzzy
breasts mistakenly removing her shawl sheathed in gold / & the
blessedness running out of time when her thighs started to keel in
the depths of a pounding psyche before turning to stone

Lorca's heavy boots all around us in that boat shop where plenty of
sun-kissed tomatoes were lying scattered here & there / their old
skin on the wane / now i looked over the lewd bridge trying to spot
the drunken boat hulking under the scaffold of lassitude / *do you
agree to take it on* / Lorca seemed to blurt out under his sombrero
/ & i was really ready to inherit his curly words that always propel
me back to a sorcery endlessly hollow & humane / how could i
forget the countenance / yet i knew the boat was waiting for me in
the dusted carmine canvas badly hung inside that rental cabin / my
fate already jettisoned

again i was about to open / or maybe i opened a jar again only
to glance down for the last time at my mistress's face soaked in
formaldehyde / luminous such a luminous face / i was raging &

not scared to laugh at my own wreck / an abscess / in her eyes i saw also our children clawing & kneading playdough / inside the kitchen of George Bush's summer home in Kennebunkport

that sun-filled slaughter house was full of Kafka & Modigliani guarding the silence of a restless gong / i tried to think of a pool of blood beat-by-beat but the oleanders kept coming back to remind me of the awaiting topsail schooner & i moved on in search of the yellow door / yellow & yellow so proud to be yellow / this is what i have always done my whole life / all i wanted was to stay put / or maybe to move to the other side of the world / where was the difference

i have never lifted my head from the lullabies to hear the cowbells the gypsy bells the queer bells the refugee bells / *are you ready* / the gong now swirling aroar through the synaptic cleft in my rodent brain / *amen* i said rising from the muddy banks of a fiction of puritanical discretion pressing creases into Donald Trump's cloak

i knew the thugs would be in power / their nobility speaking in tongues seeking that little *mariposa* / which had been perceived as poetry or pogrom of edge & edict / i could see History was wrought beneath the frippery of dovetailed blueprints of gratuitous violence / coated with old & new black blood / the crinkle flowering of kaykaykay was crowing gloriously into tomorrows / like a sop to sonnets of the lych-gate

Lorca's body will never be found

Additional Acknowledgements

My heartfelt thanks go to Natalia Spencer for her astute, incisive readings of my work in its various incarnations. I have benefited immensely from her perceptive criticism and her insightful suggestions. I am likewise grateful to Di R. Brandt for her invaluable advice on the manuscript.

My gratitude goes to Antony R. Owen, Susan Lewis, Katie Manning & Sudeep Adhikari for their interest in and support for my writing, and for taking the time to engage critically with my work.

The best outcome of this project has been in the cover art collaboration with Carol Radsprecher, an amazing Brooklyn-based artist, whose work I really admire. She listened carefully to my requests and came up with her work *Bed with Visitor* which I immediately knew would perfectly exemplify the spirit of the chapbook. I could never ask or hope for a better cover art. You are a mensch, Carol! Thanks for your unstinting support & camaraderie.

My greatest indebtedness is to my parents for their years of unyielding faith in their wayward son. Finally, but not lastly, I owe a lasting debt of gratitude to my supportive wife Arpita for always expecting nothing less than the best.

Debasis Mukhopadhyay was born in India in 1965. He spent most of his childhood in Calcutta, under the care of his maternal grandmother, who, from his early childhood, helped shape his interest in literature. As he grew up, he became a voracious and wide reader, drawn into a lifelong love affair with the written word. The rest of his childhood and adolescence was spent in small towns of West Bengal, where his father worked as a doctor in government hospitals. When Debasis was sixteen, in the throes of adolescent revolutionary idealism, he abandoned his studies and home and spent an itinerant year wandering through villages and meeting people from all walks of life. After that year, he returned home and began to channel his experiences into writing, as well as editing little magazines. The late 1980s found him back in Calcutta, where he enrolled in Alliance Française, excelling in French and then working there as a teacher and interpreter-translator for the written and audiovisual French and Francophone press. He also co-founded Polyphony, a non-profit for intercultural dialogues and transcultural communications. In 2000, he married Arpita Chakravarti, then a medical student. They moved to Canada in 2004, where he attended Université Laval, Québec, completing a PhD in literary studies in 2014.

Though Debasis had been writing poems since his Calcutta years, he did not begin submitting his poems until 2015. Since then, his poems have appeared in numerous journals and anthologies in the USA, UK, Spain & Canada, including *Posit, Words Dance, The Curly Mind, Erbacce, Strange Poetry, Yellow Cahir Review, Rat's Ass Review, The New Verse News, I Am Not A Silent Poet,*

Algebra of Owls, Mannequiin.Haüs, Of/With, Thirteen Myna Birds, Whale Road Review, Scarlet Leaf Review, With Painted Words, Writers Against Prejudice, Apple Fruits of an Old Oak, Voice of Monarch Butterflies, etc. His work has been nominated for the Best of the Net.

Debasis now lives in Montréal with his wife and son. When he is not writing, his best inspiration turns out to be what Xu Schen wrote (58 CE – ca. 147 CE): "Ink, whose semantic component is 'earth', is black."

www.ingramcontent.com/pod-product-compliance
Lightning Source LLC
LaVergne TN
LVHW051613080426
835510LV00020B/3271